SO WHAT IF ANOTHER MAN SCREWS YOUR WIFE?

A Pathway to Sexual Peace of Mind

VICTOR MEENACH

authorHOUSE®

AuthorHouse™
1663 Liberty Drive
Bloomington, IN 47403
www.authorhouse.com
Phone: 1 (800) 839-8640

Published by AuthorHouse 05/05/2017

ISBN: 978-1-5246-9074-8 (sc)
ISBN: 978-1-5246-9072-4 (hc)
ISBN: 978-1-5246-9073-1 (e)

Library of Congress Control Number: 2017906875

Print information available on the last page.

WARNING

What follows could be dangerous to your perception and opinion of yourself and others. Beware and be aware things aren't always as they seem. So be careful, chances are you're not what your think. Psychological damage could be permanent. Read and proceed at your own risk. Draw your own conclusions.

FURTHERMORE

It is well understood that a written work of this type should never be expressed in the first person. However, I am that I am and you are that you are. Consequently, there will be sections that follow which will be unconventionally just me and you.

So if you don't appreciate this approach, then don't buy the book and if you've already bought it, then ask for a refund. However, if you do, you could be missing out on a unique outlook of the male/female thing.

Dedicated to my sexy, seductive female advisor
who has had many adventurous learning experiences of her own.
Without her feminine insight, help and encouragement,
this work would not have been possible.

Pleasure

No Guilt

True Love

No Jealously

Trust

Confidence

Peace of Sexual Mind

Not in any particular order.
Seek and find herein.

Preface

Purpose: To allow monogamous true love to peacefully coexist with individual sexual freedom.

This book is written for the benefit all males and females who have suffered the abuse, jealousy, suspicion, anxiety, violence, betrayal, X divorce and just plain misery of the illusion of "one man, one woman." This insane fallacy has existed since the ancient civilizations invented and promoted it. That idea was probably a big mistake, since Homo sapiens are not genetically pair maters and rather enjoy a little variety without fear and retribution from a jealous mate or judgmental society.

Whales are pair maters, and so are most birds, particularly geese, who completely understand "what is good for the goose is good for the gander." Male humans have trouble accepting this law of nature and some females too. Whether this conflict existed in the primeval past is unknown. What is the solution to the elimination of the "battle of the sexes?"

Hopefully this work will provide perhaps controversial insights into the sexual conflicts of being a couple as well as an individual. Even more hopefully it will suggest even more controversial insights and recommendations for the solution and resolution of those conflicts, thus providing a pathway to SEXUAL PEACE OF MIND!

So What If Another Man SCREWS Your WIFE?

SO WHAT?!

Take it easy.

It might be the best thing that ever happened to you.

I am NOT

suggesting that another man screw your wife. I'm just saying "SO WHAT," if he does.

A very harsh angry emotional reaction is very preventable.

The reaction is preventable. The reality is not preventable. Read on to find out why.

Table of Contents

The War is Over

For thousands of years the human race had struggled with jealousy, spousal abuse, domestic violence, suspicion and imagined betrayal. Now men and women, lovers of every persuasion, gays, lesbians and bisexuals, have accepted their sexual, mammalian nature and instinct and can now differentiate between true love/affection and their individual sexual freedom.

Humans have finally acknowledged and accepted their sexual nature as animals. Divorce rates and domestic violence are practically nonexistent.

What was once called God's gift to man (sexual pleasure) and later perverted by society and religion has now been openly admitted, without guilt or shame or embarrassment. Human beings now realize their nudity is not a sin and have returned to a modern Garden of Eden.

We have always recognized our identity as physical beings and mental beings and spiritual beings. Finally we have acknowledged and accepted we are also sexual beings. The battle of the sexes is now finally over and both sexes have won. For the first time sexual peace of mind has been achieved.

True Confessions

I personally and unilaterally had declared a truce in the war referred to as "the battle of the sexes." I had called a peace and freed both all of the men and all of the women from the slavery of jealousy, guilt, suspicion, even resentment and hatred, not to mention sometimes violence and murder.

All had been injured in this war, some more viciously than others. Some died. Some wished they were dead. The fighting and slaughter had been going on for thousands of years. Both sides were equally powerful with counter/balancing weapons. Neither side could ever win. It was and always had been a "Mexican stand-off" "a stalemate." The slaughter and torture was relentless with both sides butchering and imprisoning the other physically and mentally. Again neither side could ever win. And now it was finally over.

At least, it was over for me. I had had enough and daringly declared the truce. It was up to me to enforce the delicate treaty, hoping that both sides would accept the wisdom of peace and understanding of the nature of life and sex. It was particularly important for me to accept "the truth" with calm and composure in my own mind. It was not an easy thing.

I was in Miami. I was thinking about my wife. I loved my wife dearly. I wanted her to have anything that made her happy. I had freed myself in the truce and wanted her to have the same freedom. I was pretty sure she didn't want that freedom and almost positive that she didn't want me to have it. Still, the war was over and I wanted to test if the peace could last, at least within me. I also was lonely and wanted the companionship of a woman.

I had heard many, many, many men, almost all other men, speak of this desire. Their testicles and hormones require that they think this way. According to them, "It doesn't mean anything." I wanted to see if that was true. I thought of my wife again. What if she was having the same thoughts? Would that be ok with me? According to the truce and treaty, it would be. I loved my wife. She was precious.

I called the escort service. It was 3 AM.

I was, still am picky. I said, "I want a blue eyed blond about 5'3' with 36C breasts who has a good sense of humor and is highly intelligent and well educated." The man says, "Just a minute." An angelic voice answered the phone. I said, "Come on over." She arrived with two muscle men that made me show my driver's license, sign a document and give them the money and left. She was wonderful, graduate of Purdue, beautiful, open minded, extremely sexual.

We tested the truce and the logic behind it. The truce and the peace held. I still loved my wife more than ever. I wanted to celebrate the peace with her. I wondered if we could.

Dominant Male Monologue

'Where the hell you been?
You should have been home five minutes ago.
Who you been talking to?
Who you been flirting with?
You know I'll beat the hell out of you if I ever catch you looking at another man.
You know I've slapped you around and beat you black and blue before.'

Hey Joe, I said where you goin' with that gun in your hand?
Alright. I'm goin down to shoot my old lady,
you know I caught her messin' 'round with another man.
Yeah,! I'm goin' down to shoot my old lady,
you know I caught her messin' 'round with another man.
Huh! And that ain't too cool.

—Jimi Hendrix, "Hey Joe"

Man has his woman
To take his seed
He's got the power
She's got the need
Only women bleed
Only women bleed

—Alice Cooper, "Only Women Bleed"

Stop the bleeding.
Men can bleed too.
Stop all of it.

Modern Canterbury Tale and Other Stuff

"A tale told by an idiot" — Shakespeare
I worked with a guy and over time got to know him, then he told me this story. He and his wife went to a disco together. (Does anybody remember DISCO?) They were sitting at the bar together, when another woman approached him and began flirting and talking to him. (Bring back disco!) He was a good looking guy and enjoyed the attention. All men enjoy female attention. In fact, they're suckers for it. Women enjoy attention also. All humans enjoy sexual attention.

The innocent and maybe not innocent flirting and conversation continued, with his wife attempting to eavesdrop. He never introduced them. He danced a couple of times with the other woman. Then, he and his wife left for home. The conversation on the way home was sparse. He felt a little bit guilty and a little bit not guilty. He wondered what his wife was thinking.

Upon arriving inside their home, she enlightened him. He said she went into an uncontrollable jealous violent rage, cussing him in all manner of unspeakable terms. She began crying and screaming and flailing at him. She ran into their bedroom and brought a pistol out and shot herself in the head in front of him.

Hey Joe, my lady shot HERSELF down, thought I might be capable of messing around!

The whole world says it's cheating.....but maybe not

Axioms number 1 and 2:
1. True love is sacred
2. Sexual fantasy is animal lust and instinctually hot
Logical assumption: the two combined equals a symbolic molecule of true lover's bliss.
She said, 'What a great orgasm, I can't wait to get home and tell my husband about it!'
He said, 'I hope my wife had an exciting encounter today, I can't wait to get home and have her tell me all about it!'
Is monogamous promiscuity possible or a contradiction?
Are they true lovers or freaky kinky sex addicts?
Or ….. have they achieved sexual peace of mind?

It didn't mean anything — true or false?

It didn't mean anything, says the man: mostly true
It didn't mean anything, says the woman: who knows?
Men assume it did mean something to the woman and go crazy!
Both men and women almost always go crazy!
What a waste especially if there are children.
The Etruscans, Bali, Greek, Roman, some African and pagan cultures promoted sexual freedom. They understood and accepted and differentiated sexual pleasure from true love and true caring.
NO BIG DEAL
Immaturity, insecurity and jealousy--what a drag!!!!!

Unlike a Rose, Jealousy by Any Other Name Smells as Bad

a tale told by an idiot
the male and female game
full of sound and fury
mixed with guilt and shame

signifying something but
no one knows for sure
union is quite compelling
but marriage not a cure

love is not an answer
friendship not a clue
opposite sex together
cannot know what's true

lying with each other
sharing strange delight
when the sharing's over
an ugly resentment fight

passion is a killer
cutting blade of pain
double edged horror
love/hate both insane

burning with hot desire
to capture true love's crest
blazing with inner fire
questioning fidelity's test

the male, a violent hero
protecting his beauty queen
from all other undertakings
an unnatural perverted scene

the female yields consenting
to her man's insistent approach
until it's too unrelenting
too painful for him to encroach

upon her greater beauty
upon her mind and soul
and can no longer bear
his same solitary goal
of constant preoccupation
with only him and she
for completely total capture
not even a moment free

she then seeks other options
makes excuses to do this and that
she flees the smothering prison
wants to kill the miserable rat

he hates, they both hate equally
the revenge plot goes on and on
what was once is now the opposite
great euphoria of oneness gone

it's a weird tale told by an idiot
heard way too many times before
the plight of the sensual lovers
the jealous man, his imagined whore

— By the author

Monogamous Equations

True or False?

Love does not equal sex or vice versa.

Sex does not equal cheating.

Orgasm does not equal love.

True love plus suspicion equals conflict.

Suspicion multiplied by jealousy equals emotional chaos.

True love can equal sexual freedom and emotional peace of mind.

Sexuality equals spirituality.

The Hindu Tantra may provide some insights and will be detailed later.

In the meantime.......take it easy.......don't go crazy...don't ever go crazy!!!

Men are Skum...(they can't help it)

It's that they're born with the law of nature's genetics.

Their testosterone hormone governs their subconscious instruction, leading to a strong tendency to promiscuous behavior....plus men are weak, actually very weak and suckers for temptation.

If not, why is prostitution the oldest profession?

Women might even be bigger suckers in a different way. Again, who knows?

No matter! Sexuality is the strongest instinct of the human race and all other life species. It insures continuation of the species.

It's a double standard, but men have always felt justified. Why? Because it usually doesn't mean anything...it's genetic instruction.

Men say "look at those breasts, look at that ass, look at those legs" (Note, men never say look at that hair.)

Oral sex is not sexual relations....where has that been heard before?

Conquest, pursuit, seduction.....does rooster, bull, stud sound familiar? None of them can help it. It's their job. The females accept it. It's their job.

Are humans animals? As much as the human race tries to deny it, they are animals and as such have the same instincts. However, as human animals suffering from guilt, shame and embarrassment stemming from religion and social conditioning, they go crazy about sexual jealousy. Take it easy. Don't go crazy!

What the hell?

"IF" one thinks this work is only about sex, then how WRONG could one be???

However, one could be right about that, or maybe could be right and wrong!!!..... What the hell?

Or, is this work about spirituality?

Is the goal of sexual gratification good for both true lovers, or not?

What the hell for sure!

The true lovers don't have to do anything...just knowing comfortably that both are free to be natural individual sexual beings. To be able to discuss it honestly together without jealousy is glorious.

Is the author promoting swinging, group sex, perversion of every kind? Maybe...whatever turns one on.

Sexual peace of mind is a treasure. What is the path? The current and historical path leads to the wilderness of jealousy and abuse, UGH!

A Miraculous Tale with a Bad Ending

I met a woman at the post office and opened the door for her. I looked into her eyes and felt like I had known her for a million years. It was love at first sight. The Beatles asked "Do you believe in love at first sight? Yes, I'm certain that it happens all the time."

I couldn't wait to get home and call her, discovering she felt the same way. It was perfect. She lived just four blocks from me, congruent with Hugh Heffner's "the girl next door theory." We arranged to meet later that night at her house. Mutual trust was immediately established.

She was as uninhibited, open-minded and as free thinking as me. We rubbed each other's feet, kissed, touched and exchanged personal stories, experiences and adventures with each trying to outdo the other. Once again, it was perfect! We progressed on all levels for two weeks. It was a "Happening."

Then, as Murphy's Law always prevails, she suddenly and secretly sold her house much to my objection. Her jealous and abusive ex-husband had beaten her and thrown her up against walls crushing four vertebras. He had done that many years ago, but now as she aged, the pain was getting worse and worse. She was accepted into a pain clinic in Tennessee where her son lives. (By the way, it's difficult to get into a pain clinic. Most are full.) I wonder how full a sexual-emotional pain clinic would be. I never saw her again.

A One in a Million Tale

Two true lovers lay in a safe warm bed, cuddled lovingly, secure in the knowledge and trust that absolutely nothing could interfere with their oneness. They exchanged sexual fantasies freely. She wanted him to experience and enjoy his manhood. Summarily, he wanted her to explore and enjoy her womanhood, both understanding individual freedom and human nature. They loved each other! They laughed and played, sometimes together, sometimes apart, but always never betraying their oneness.

They relished and frolicked in their sexual peace of mind. And all was good.
Imaginative Etcetera of a Plural Good Time
man and a woman
Apollo and Venus
Twin energy of eros's
Power to redeem us

God and the goddess
rulers of the night
mysteries of beauty
filled with delight

unselfish sharing
between the two lovers
adventure and daring
the couple discovers

the pathway to heaven
a road to their throne
with freedom and giving
together, not alone

one's care for the other
an understanding of nature
not afraid of experiment
or a flirtatious refresher

male and the female
researching new joy
recapturing their youth
as a girl and a boy

magic of innocence
lost in old time
knowing its wonder but
missing its rhyme

wanting to treasure
the bliss of the past
seeking a measure to
assure this will last

fond in the hope
they can reap it together
rekindle both's thrill
through a mutual endeavor
not forsaking their union
but adding a strange twist
to aide in the excitement
of fantasies they've kissed

realizing love and emotion
to be different from lust
that passion and pleasure
does not betray trust

*two super sharp people
from an unknown turf
with courage to pursue
an imaginative rebirth*

— By the author

Fragments of the Hindu Tantra

Tantra is where.....sexuality and spiritually are the same thing.

There is more to Tantra than that, including Kundalini, a very powerful sex force.

Yoni loves Onk!

Which loosely translated.....means genitals love genitals!!!

"What's wrong with that?" a silly love song by Paul McCartney.

Appropriate sexual behavior depends on which culture, society, or religion you believe in. Don't believe in anything. "The beginning of belief is the end of all knowledge." Goethe

An old tradition in Eskimoland: When a male friend visits a man's lodge, the guest sleeps with his friend's wife. Guess who likes that? The man, the guest and the wife.

Carve nothing in stone.

Pleasure......What a Joy!

Pleasure is perhaps the highest good, the pinnacle of spiritual worship, the ultimate compliment to the Creator.

> The taste of a juicy steak or buttered lobster
> The sound of a symphonic orchestra
> The sight of majestic mountains or a seashore sunset
> The ecstasy of an exciting intense orgasm

Which of the above is forbidden except under certain circumstances and with a whole bunch of social rules and enigmas? and WHY?

Do those boundaries induce peace of mind? Yes, maybe in some ways (monogamous fidelity), maybe not (monogamous promiscuity) in others. Is there an answer? maybe, maybe not. If so, is it jealousy? Is it self-inflicted guilt? Is it secret self-indulgence? Could the "lovers" enjoy all manners of pleasure together? "been searching so long, to find an answer" — Rock Band, Chicago

Why not enjoy your **body** while you're alive? Does that mean with just one person?
Why not enjoy your **soul** while you're alive? Does that mean with just one person?

One Night Stand

If you haven't had one, you haven't lived. You learn all the glory and all the horror of pure raw sex. It's meaningless, especially afterward. And it's especially horrifying if you are in love with your true love waiting at home for you. Still, there is an almost irresistible thrill to chance the risk. It's an animal thing, an instinct and nothing at all to be jealous about. The true lovers should understand this and not be threatened.

This is much easier said than done. One night stands were very popular in the 70's before hideous diseases, guilt propaganda, strip clubs, internet pornography and cell phones, where your true love expects you to answer. The true lovers both know about this temptation and could decide what's good or bad for one is good or bad for the other. It's a difficult decision and should be discussed honestly. (Remember the Eskimos).

Remember the praying mantis and the black widow spider, where the male is willing to die for one sexual encounter with the seductive female. Remember "men are scum"). Remember, women like it too. Remember we are animal sexual beings. Take it easy. Don't go crazy. Don't ever go crazy, especially if you love your sweetheart. If you don't, you neither should be together. If you do, why not allow each other a little individual freedom. It easily could embellish your love together, especially if you tell each other the juicy details. You might be pleasantly surprised!

Bring back the One Night Stands, openly without all the secrets and deception.

Philandering

Ever hear of a harem? It's normal for mammalian alpha male instinct. But......it might be more fun to be a eunuch, who really got the good stuff.

Mother nature is extremely promiscuous. Ain't it grand? And she consequently propagated life and beauty across the entire earth.

Monogamous promiscuity......Is it a contradiction or quite logical and makes perfect sense?

Dare to be honest. Dare to communicate. Dare to act. Your partner will either love you for it or divorce you.

Is all the drama necessary?

Wife swapping

Is wife swapping a good idea? Do you swap with friends or swap with strangers? Either way, it's probably not a good idea. It can be way too personal.

Remember Bob, Carol, Ted, and Alice. That did not turn out very well. Maybe if the couples switched and then went to different locations, it might work a lot better.

Once again, it might work perfect, if the true love's just imagined it privately by themselves. And also once again, that suggestion has been the overriding theme of this book.

Sharing each other's animal lust and desire, is the "Ticket to Paradise!"

Classic Lover's Dialogue

(He Said, She Said)

Husband to wife: "If I ever catch you with another man, I'll kill you."

Wife to husband: "If I ever catch you with another woman, I'll kill you."

With regard to this typical reaction, "kill" refers not only to actual murder, but can also be translated as intense hatred, extreme violence, verbal and physical abuse, all manner of rage, divorce and other ugly behavior. In other words, whether he said or she said, it's the end of their loving relationship together.

Picky, picky, picky.

There should have been eight deadly sins. They left out jealousy. Jealousy is the leading cause of spousal murder.

Seldom Heard Lover's Dialogue

(He Said, She Said)

Husband to wife: "I love you baby. I want you to freely enjoy your feminine sexuality."

Wife to husband: "I love you baby. I want you to freely enjoy your masculine sexuality."

With regard to these atypical assertions, "love" refers not only to the trusting bond between the two lovers, but can also indicate lasting unity, pure affection, mutual understanding and one's appreciation and respect for the other's sexual individuality. In other words, whether he said or she said, the two exist in total harmony with complete sexual peace of mind.

Kissy, kissy, kissy.

Axioms

Number One: a scared man can't gamble ... successfully

Number Two: a jealous man can't work ... productively

If the reader plays poker, blackjack, roulette, dice, etc., they will know exactly what "Number One" means and know it to be oh so true!

As for "Number Two," the man is distracted, always thinking about who's flirting with and/or propositioning his wife. He's wondering if she can be seduced by who's hitting on her, because he knows for absolutely sure that some man or possibly woman sooner or later will be. It's the law of nature. Depending on his level of jealousy, he can't wait till he gets home and gives her the third degree or maybe even beats her up if his imagination goes crazy. It happens.

Jealousy doesn't have to be the conditioned law not society. Why not accept the true law of nature "genitals love genitals" and deal with it in trust and love.

The Mind, the Soul and the Body

If you could have two out of three of the above from your lover, which two would you choose?

Hookers, Call Girls, Strippers and other Rent a Sex

Add to the above categories: pornography, X and R rated movies, television shows and advertising, racy magazines, artificial devices, romance novels, Viagra, Victoria's Secret and other lingerie etc. Together it is a multi-billion dollar industry. WHY? Is it because there is huge demand, from an insatiable hunger for sexual gratification? Obviously, it is.

It is impossible to over estimate how much humans think about SEX!!!

Some research suggests that the majority of adult humans think about SEX, in one way or another, approximately 80 percent of their time.

Sexual Tension, Curiosity and Desire

They are everywhere: walking down the street, at work, meetings, watching TV, listening to music, alone and only with the inner mind. All three exist without relief. Perhaps only old age combats IT, but even then IT still lingers. The glory and agony of sexuality goes on. There is no defense. One way or another, it's hideous/angelic face forces the human instinct to succumb. The force is relentless, disguising itself as love, security, intimacy, friendship, companionship and maybe just admitting pure pleasure. No matter what, the quest and torture is unending.

New love is a defense, but not reliable. True love is a better defense and occasionally withstands the barrage at least physically, but whoever knows what lurks within the mind. Who knows the secret thoughts and fantasies of both male and female? Men's are more predictable and whoever knows what women are thinking? Women are mysterious and a large part of the allure. Notwithstanding, the sexual game goes on, nobody knowing what anybody is thinking or doing, but always at least a little bit suspicious, since everybody knows the facts of life, the birds and the bees, the flowers and trees, the sweet nectar of life. Why not accept the inevitable and enjoy the infinite possibilities with someone you love???

Some More Dialogue

She said "Hey honey, I'm going to buy some strange sex today."

He said "You sure it's safe?"

She said "Yeah, I checked it out."

He said "You'll tell me about it won't you?"

She said "Absolutely."

He said "Then can we make love afterward?"

She said "Absolutely."

She said "Why do you think I'm doing this?"

He said "For me?"

She said "Absolutely!"

He said "I love you baby!"

She said "I love you completely always have always will."

He said "Kiss me."

She did. He felt her and she was wet. He loved her so.

The Garden of Eden

What a drag! There was no one to cheat with. At first, this was no problem no problem. The newness of opposite sexuality provided many pleasures and much excitement until after years of constant nudity their familiarity bred contempt. And after thousands and thousands of orgasms since there was nothing else to do, it became boring, boring.

They still loved each other very much and were great companions easing any loneliness.
However, their desire diminished daily. The snake helped a little, telling eve of different realities and other worlds of mind. Eve was cool and couldn't wait to share the new carnal knowledge with Adam, because she loved him dearly.

Adam was hesitant at first, but didn't feel threatened or jealous since there were no other men for eve to fool around with. So.... they both enjoyed it in their minds. Eventually Adam got the idea and began to fantasize about other non-existent women. Their love, trust, honesty and desire for each other were renewed. It was hot and they shared it together in perfect peace and harmony.

Then god got pissed off and kicked them out, which was very good for them and the future of all humanity, except most humans never understood the true nature of sexuality the way Eve and Adam did.

Before and After the Garden

Before the first time sex in the garden there was primal lust, desire, anticipation; after the first time there was hopefully intimacy, true love, trust, sacred union and of course anticipation for the second time, third time, fourth time and on and on and better and better. Before and after, they were in paradise together.

Before and after the three thousandth time, they wished for the first time again, for the very first time, to quote a song. But how? To experience first time excitement, "Before and after" could be the rule, the one and only rule. Tell each other before and after any wild adventure and enjoy it together!

It will very possibly be like the first time every time, if the two true lovers trust each other and openly share their secret fantasies. Whether it works out or not, it sure beats jealousy, mistrust, resentment and boring, boring. Before and after is sexual peace of mind.

Pleasures of the Flesh

It is sometimes known as the forbidden fruit.

Is it a sin to enjoy this fruit? It is a very sweet fruit indeed. It grows on the "tree of life."
The fruit hangs ripe to be plucked by all who hunger for physical and perhaps spiritual nourishment and renewal. Its taste and texture is divine, literally and symbolically. It provides the essence of life's energy, as well as the seed of continuation.

Some religions regard it as a sinful ingestion and an evil temptation to the body and the soul. These religions regard knowledge much the same way. Other religions praise it as a pathway to heaven. Perhaps, the fruit can be both or neither, depending on how it's prepared. Unfortunately, most times, like vengeance, it's considered best served cold. Fortunately, others prefer it to be hot when eaten and understand the difference.

Nevertheless, the fruit grows everywhere in abundance and may be the most powerful energy source in the Universe, capable of burning or nourishing all who partake. The fruit is not only natural, but virtually irresistible. Its' nutrition sustains all life. It should never be blamed for the indigestion of guilt and/or jealousy. Consume it freely and often. Bon appetit!

"All you need is love." — The Beatles

Does being in love guarantee the right to be jealous???

What is the lover in love with? The body?, The mind?, The soul?, The sense of humor, the bank account, the credit card, the income, the food, the security? Or is the lover in love with the convenient pleasure? Is the lover in love with, as George Bernard Shaw said, "the exaggerated difference between one person and everybody else?" No matter, who wouldn't be jealous of all of that? Who wouldn't want to control it, protect it? Why would that be required?

Is that what "in love" is? Maybe it is, maybe not. Does "being in love" mean wanting to provide those things? Regardless, "all you need is love," whatever it is. As they say, "it's all good!" What is not needed however is jealousy, guilt and abuse. What is needed is individual freedom and complete honesty, no matter how sensitive. Share the truth of the inner selves to discover if it's truly "in love." Share the conspiracy of two lovers "against the world" "against the wind."

All you need is love, real love!

The Submissive
(believe it or not)

There are women and some men that love to be controlled and verbally abused in the guise of love and the violence of jealousy. They love to be yelled at, slapped and spanked. It turns them on. It's a phenomenon. They may flirt and play with others just to invoke a reaction. It turns the dominant on also. In some instances, it may be considered true love. It can be cool!

In other cases, the exact same circumstances exist. Yet, the result is hideous and brutal real jealousy and violence. The dominant is only insecurity personified. The submissive is only submitting to fear. Neither is turned on. Both resent each other.

The tendency of jealousy exists in all relationships. Take it easy! Enjoy each other.

Question: No doubt, people do like this type of treatment (just look at the popularity of books like *Shades of Grey*), either first hand or vicariously. But why? Why would anyone want to be verbally or physically abused? How can this be love? Is it love or something else?

Response: It's hot, produces powerful orgasms and promotes a unique sense of private oneness.

Can It Be Imagined?

A society, civilization, culture, belief system where any two consenting adults, sexually attracted to each other are free without guilt, criticism, judgment, or any retribution to enjoy pure impersonal physical pleasure at will? The Etruscans in Roman times almost achieved it. Studio 54 in New York did achieve it in the 70's. It was called faceless sex. Both understood the outlet for animal nature and lust and condoned it.

Is it possible to imagine? Would it be psychologically healthy?

Question: Under what circumstances, if any, would you do this when married?

Response: The purpose is to differentiate between sex and true love commitment in an effort to eliminate jealousy and negative consequences.

Question: Social norms don't stop some people from having free sex, but it would be hard to imagine society as a whole accepting this. What more could you say to convince everyone?

Response: I'm not concerned about convincing anyone, rather only presenting drastic alternative ideas of thinking.

Outer Space, Heaven, or the Great Beyond

Assume/imagine individual consciousness after individual death. Imagine being alone with no physical body, just memories. How one would yearn for the taste of food, the smell of the ocean, the sound of music, the pleasure of a heart pounding orgasm. Would there be regrets for petty jealousies and abuse, especially for someone loved?

Would there be regrets for many missed sexual adventures, not only for the individual, but as well as the one loved (the true love partner), perhaps together and if it weren't real bodily adventures, would it be regrets of the mind shared by both in the spirit of honesty? Would one yearn for a body, for just one day to truly without inhibition or social conditioning to experience their human sexuality? The individual was taught from birth to be afraid of that. Why?

Imagine eternity with no way back, no physical body to connect with the 5 senses. Imagine what could have been. Imagine the peace of mind void of jealousy and insecurity. Imagine the goodwill and freedom extended to all, especially a true love and enjoyed by the individual as well. Imagine it now, before it's too late.

Genitals Verses Brains

Are genitals a second brain or are they the primary brain? Women have accused men of thinking with their genitals for years. And ... they might be right. Maybe ... both sexes should think with their genitals and give up all the jealousy, anxiety, suspicion, guilt and sexual conflict that the logical socially conditioned "big" brain produces.

"I struggle against myself" Lancelot said in Excalibur, after stabbing himself over his lust for Guinevere as opposed to his genuine loyalty to the king. If king Arthur, Lancelot and Guinevere all thought with their genitals and truly understood and freely accepted the nature of mammalian human sexuality, maybe Camelot would not only not have been a tragedy, but rather an even greater concept of "what can be."

Situational ethics are always in play and governed by the socially conditioned "big" brain daddy who says, "shame on you" or NO..."shame on you." Or worse still..."shame on them." When it comes to sex, shame should be in there someplace, not to mention guilt and fear and jealousy! Take it easy. Accept the genital brain for what it is, not to be confused with love and affection, nor to be condemned for betrayal automatically. Both brains working together without conflict in honest communication with a true love is highly recommended.

Standard Procedure

She's 15 minutes late. He's getting pissed off. She drove a friend across town at the last minute because of her friend's car problem. She's 30 minutes late and he's really getting pissed off. He's too cheap to buy her a cell phone. She's 45 minutes late now and he's going crazy with suspicion and mistrust. Don't ever go crazy. She finally arrives.

Scenario 1: he questions her relentlessly. Where you been? Who you been with? Who is he? He doesn't believe her explanation and doesn't speak to her the rest of the night.

Scenario 2: he asks the exact same questions. Then he shakes her hard. He cusses her and then slaps the hell out of her.

An Ounce of Prevention is Worth a Pound of Cure

Avoidance may equal wisdom and future security. Two possible true lovers first meet. Sparks fly. Pheromones and endorphins abound. Mental ecstasy, imagination and possibility flourish. It's possibly the most wonderful feeling in life! They obviously will love each other forever.

However, danger lurks. Most times, the lovers are too giddy in the present to acknowledge the future. Why not enjoy the beauty of the present? However again, why not have a conversation and understanding ahead of time regarding what has haunted couples from the beginning?

He says, "I love you completely. You are so beautiful and desirable. And I know that there will many other men hitting on you and flirting with you every day. I also know you will like that. It's natural. It may also happen with me also and I'll like it. It's just the way IT is. Let's not let that divide us with jealousy. Let's uninhibitedly enjoy that fact and enjoy our inner sexual selves together.

She says, "I agree completely. We'll have so much fun expressing our secret honest sexual desires without fear. I love you!"

Cats and Dogs Dialogue

"Did you ever visit someone and they had a strange unknown cat or dog or both or more?"

"Yes."

"Did you immediately want to pet it or both of them or all of them?"

"Yes."

"Cats and dogs love to be touched and petted."

"Did the touch feel good to both you and the animal/s?"

"Absolutely"

"Then why wouldn't strange men and women want to touch and pet each other?"

"Why wouldn't they touch and pet each other without guilt or apprehension just like other animals?"

"That is if they both wanted to."

"What are the odds they do?"

"Maybe even your wife. Maybe even you."

One, Two, Three...Maybe Four, Maybe More

Try it, you may like it. If not, it will at least give you and your partner something new and exciting to talk about—a great conversation piece. It may also provide a new perspective and supplemental identity to embark on a completely new adventure.

Do I try this with friends or strangers? A recommendation is with strangers. Remember the disaster of Bob, Ted, Carol and Alice. If you choose friends, beware of the danger. However, any forbidden adventure will render its lessons and wisdom.

This experiment will yield results whether you actually do it or just talk about it. Regardless, it will open new pathways of understanding and tend to reduce jealousy between you and your partner.

Just do it and proceed to mutual joy and trust without jealousy at all.

The Male Female Thing, the Difference and the Purpose

In all of nature, the difference is the same—it's physiological. In all of nature, except humans, the purpose is the same: procreation and continuation of the species. Nature is simple. Humans are not.

The human male/female thing is extremely more complex. What is the purpose? Obviously a primary purpose is also procreation and continuation of the species. However, the human male/female thing serves many other purposes. These include pleasure, ego, self-confidence, excitement, adventure, companionship, shared laughter, prosperity, intimacy, social activities, intellectual stimulation, security, encouragement, reinforcement, mutual-grooming, family and shared memories. The list goes on.

Why would any intelligent human allow jealousy and the accompanying vengeance and resentment, hatred, anger and abuse to jeopardize these joys and benefits over a little meaningless sexual curiosity and attention? Everyone loves attention and everyone is curious. Why make a mountain out of a molehill?

What is the other difference? It may be more significant than the other purposes. The difference is cultural conditioning that all are trained to be and to behave from birth. The Greeks killed their female babies on Mount Olympus. Eskimos share their wives with guests. Arabs have harems. Catholics forbid contraception. Mormons have multiple wives. The Amazon women in South America ruled all. The priestesses in Scandinavia also ruled the men in sexual matters. Pagans allowed and encouraged total sexual freedom. Western civilizations prefer chauvinism, repression, and suppression of sexual behavior. Choose wisely!

Sex is not necessarily a betrayal. If it was, they wouldn't have made skirts, high heels, lipstick, and low cut blouses.

Take it easy. Enjoy the entire package TOGETHER.

Mark Twain

"Letters from Earth"

In this short story, Twain created a plot in which, three archangels Michael, Gabriel and Lucifer conspired humorously in heaven behind God's back. Occasionally, God would get mad at Lucifer, who was the ringleader and the original "Peck's bad boy." At those times, God would banish Lucifer into cold dark space for thousands of years.

But, this time God had just created the universe and the Earth with it, along with life. So, instead of the cold dark space thing, Lucifer decided to visit the Earth. He wrote letters back to Michael and Gabriel in heaven informing them of what he found.

He found many strange things, the strangest of which, were humans. He knew Michael and Gabriel would be very amused at their customs. One custom that was particularly strange was their behavior, concerning sexuality.

He pointed out that males were allowed to have at least one mistress, maybe more. Rich males could have harems and slave girls. The reason this seemed so strange to him was that one man could not even satisfy one woman; whereas, one woman could satisfy at least 10 men maybe 50.

He questioned the logic of this insane double standard and why it was taboo for women to have multiple partners.
However, he did not propose a solution. I am proposing one now, at least an alternative way of thinking.

Being

Let's see, I am a physical being and a mental being and a spiritual being. What have I left out? Oh yeah, I am a sexual being. Why am I ashamed and afraid of that?

If I am a woman, I know full well why I am afraid. It's the constant unrelenting social pressure to be a good girl. I am programed from birth not to enjoy my GIFT.

My gift can be my true Love's gift also, if he could only understand that. But he is jealous and possessive and ruins it for everybody. Snakes have orgies and dolphins too. Romans had Grand orgies and the Etruscans and pagans even grander. What happened? Oh, I forgot we are more civilized now.

So instead of enjoying our entire being, we keep those type sexual thoughts hidden and locked away behind the Great Wall of the Mind.

Wilhelm Reich wrote several books insisting that sexual repression and suppression was the cause of disease in our physical being. They burned his books in Boston. I am not sure if that is true, but I can only imagine how it affects us mentally and spiritually.

Of course, orgies are the extreme. But Freud was convinced that whenever two people are making love, at least four people are involved, indicating that each of the two were having their own private fantasy in their mind.

Why deny it? We all know it's true. Why not enjoy it and live it with your true love?

Orgies

The author is not necessarily suggesting that you actually attend an orgy. Instead why not, as a couple, have an imaginary one in your heads together.

A Nude Beach

can be quite an enlightening learning experience. There are lots of nude people walking and laying around unashamed and not embarrassed by their nudity. They are proud of the way they were created. Why not be?

It is more exciting and more enjoyable to take your mate with you. However, it is not an erotic stimulation. It is more of an intellectual and spiritual adventure. It promotes an acceptance of what we are and without interference from the Great Wall of the Mind.

Here, it is the body we display uninhibitedly. It is a very liberating experience, very liberating indeed. It can be a good start on a pathway to sexual peace of mind.

Nudity extended

Why do humans wear clothes? Other than shoes, to keep warm, or protection from the weather, there is really no reason they should have to.

There are some benefits however. They provide a place to keep a wallet, car keys and other paraphernalia. Clothes also can show status, authority, identity etc. But there is really no reason to make clothes mandatory. That should have been included in the Bill of Rights.

I say if you want to wear clothes wear them. If you don't want to wear clothes, don't wear them. How in the world is there a market for pajamas?

Nudist colonies and camps are more of a turn off than a turn on. Like the nude beach, they provide more of a spiritual experience and an opportunity to meet other people of like mind.

There is a theory that humans invented clothes in order to make the male/female sex thing more exciting. They got bored seeing nakedness all of the time. So, they put nudity in the forbidden and taboo category to spice things up and create a little mystery. It worked.

By placing nudity in the no-no category, the mystery of the opposite sex captivates everyone's attention. Clothes are now an aphrodisiac.

"Seen one, seen them all" is a thing of the past.

The Garden of Eden ...Revisited

God visited ADAM AND EVE in the garden with two gifts, one for each. He said "I have two gifts. You can choose which one you want. The first gift is the ability to stand up and pee." Adam spoke up and exclaimed
"that sounds so neat and cool, I'll take that one." God said, "ok Eve you get multiple orgasms."

It is well known to what extents men will go for just that one orgasm; anywhere from blow up dolls to plastic hand-held vaginas, hookers, strip clubs, massage parlors, rape, kidnapping and who knows?

Men will jeopardize their reputations, careers, Financial Security, true love relationship, health via disease, "life and limb" getting conned, robbed, or even killed. It is almost as extreme as the male praying mantis and black widow, who know for sure they are going to die. What a powerful animal instinct!

AND

It is easy to understand why the woman at work, the girl at the bar, or any friendly woman in a social setting is a much safer alternative to satisfy the Raging Beast, Desperately Seeking that one orgasm.

BUT

What about "EVE?" who can achieve multiple orgasms, one after the other after the other and on and on. What desire and motivation she must have. Scientists say that in the entire Animal Kingdom only the female homosapien has the ability for orgasms. It has been called God's gift to mankind.

I say let her use it anyway she wants. As her true love, you will enjoy it also and it will eliminate all of those risk aspects mentioned above.

A reminder to the reader and to the author:

This book is NOT intended to promote promiscuity, but rather, to encourage honest open dialogue between the true lovers. Wouldn't it be nice (as the Beach Boys sang) to share the deepest darkest forbidden lustful animal desires and fantasies of your soulmate?

That is a daring risk and one few are willing to take. Yet it could be, not only a pathway to sexual peace of mind, but a grand opportunity for thrilling adventures together, whether real or imagined, it does not matter. What does matter is that the two are now truly one with nothing to hide.

By the way

In our modern culture, marriage is a legal proposition with all kinds of laws, rules, rights, ceremonies, and even expectations.

In the ancient Greek and Latin languages, marriage was simply defined as two people deciding to live together.

Open Marriage

Some readers may think I am advocating open marriage.

WRONG!!!

Open marriage seldom works simply because an agreement is far different from a true sharing. An agreement allows each other sexual freedom, but rarely do either of them discuss the details and usually keep their escapades secret.

It's better than nothing, but far less than my proposal. It still leaves open the grounds for suspicion, betrayal, deceit, and worry about your partner's true intentions.

Open marriage is emotionally dangerous. It is the murky middle ground between total silence of what is sexually instinctive and the total trusting oneness of the soulmates. I am advocating what I call "monogamous promiscuity."

Divorce

What an excruciatingly painful experience divorce is, especially if there are children! Just a break up is bad enough.

Admittedly, there may be legitimate reasons for divorce, such as continued abuse, domestic violence, ideological differences, growing to hate each other and so on.

However, what is called "sexually unfaithful" is NOT one of them. Hell, everyone has been doing that in their mind from the beginning.

Now, "emotionally unfaithful" is a far different story and could be a legitimate reason for divorce. But, to automatically jump to that conclusion because of a sexual escapade is not justified.

All of this pain might be avoided by accepting and understanding the "law of sexual nature," instead of trying to deny it after marriage.

Denying one's instinctive animal nature and the instinctive nature of their chosen mate produces conflict, guilt, suspicion, jealousy and maybe divorce Why not freely accept and admit each others' sexual nature, programmed into the DNA and enjoy the truth of it.

Now there is a marriage made in heaven!

Chimpanzee nature

Chimpanzees live in highly socialized separate tribes. Occasionally, a female chimpanzee will sneak off to another tribe and have sex with several males there and then sneak back. That is their nature.

Similarly, it is also Human Nature for both males and females to enjoy some variety. After all variety is the spice of life.
But, why do humans need to sneak? Obviously, it is because of social mores, customs, and age-old conditioning. Fear of retribution and negative social consequences are also high on the list.

No modern society has gotten appropriate sexual behavior right. Japan and Hindu India, along with some European countries and some Island cultures are far more lenient in their sexual thinking. And for sure, don't forget the Eskimos.

Don't shame on me.

The Scarlet Letter

What a puritanical concept that is. The Bible says that sex is God's gift to mankind. The question is if it is a gift, why can't mankind use It anyway mankind wants without shame, provided the act is consensual?

And why is God always put in the sexual equation? I don't know about you, but when I give a gift I don't tell them how to use it, when to use it, when not to use it or not to use it at all. I don't specify a bunch of rules concerning the gift.

I don't think God did that either. I think men did that for their own selfish purpose.
It's hard to believe that God wrapped his gift in shame and fear and guilt paper. And it's even harder to believe that he didn't intend for it to be enjoyed equally. Equally is the key word here.

Duty calls

Compare this to that.

Men frequently say the worst I ever had was great!

Women frequently say the best I ever had was awful!

My grandma told my mom just before my mom got married, that it was going to be her duty to satisfy her husband sexually. She added..... but you won't like it.

Since then, times have probably changed, but maybe not. Certainly, almost any product for sale has sexual innuendo advertising attached to it. Women have joined the hunt. They may enjoy being the predator instead of the prey.

Nonetheless, the sex act may still seem more of a duty than a pleasure to many couples. What a waste compared to what it can be.

Has anyone, male or female, ever faked an orgasm just to complete their Duty and get it over with?

Mathematic sexual equations

Man plus Woman equals continuation of the species

Man minus Woman equals extreme loneliness

Man divided by Woman equals conflict and frustration

Man multiplied by Woman equals euphoric BLISS

Hardcore jealousy — domestic violence — needless divorce

Take it easy!!! Don't go crazy!!! Don't ever go crazy!!!

Mount Olympus gods and goddesses suffered from jealousy, the most famous of which, was Hera. I prefer Voltaire by far.

Jealousy-The Green Eyed Monster of Bad Physical Health

Wilhelm Reich researched the physical effects of sexual suppression and repression in the early 1900's. He concluded that those attitudes could cause cancer and other maladies in the body.

He a reasoned that such attitudes and behavior disrupted the body's energy field, consequently clogging up vital life processes.

Today, many medical and scientific researchers are linking negative emotions to bad physical health. Jealousy and the stress that comes with it is the number one culprit.

You will have to Google the expert details on your own. I am not qualified to explain them properly. But, this will give you a heads up. Google jealousy also. What you find might amaze you.

Don't go crazy! Don't ever go crazy. Jealousy is preventable. Laughter may be an excellent replacement.

And please don't forget monogamous promiscuity!

How do women think and what?

Whoever knows what a woman is thinking???
And why is she thinking it?

Would her man really want to know??? It could be scary, even frightening.

The way she dresses is an indication of her inner thoughts. She often wears dresses, short skirts, tight shorts, high heels, revealing bikinis. The list goes on.

She puts on lipstick, makeup, earrings, perfume. Everything about her is alluring and seductive. She wears her femininity and sensuality on her sleeve, so to speak.

She says she wants to look good for her man. She wants him to be proud of her. I, for one, believe her. It could also mean that she desires to express her total sexuality with her man in a secret sacred union of unbridled lust.

The possibilities between them are endless!

Rumor Has It

I do not know if this is true, but I have heard through the grapevine that women are turning more and more to women for a true partnership. One reason for this is that men are so kindergarten thinking about sexuality.

Again, I tend to believe this. Since after randomly listening to thousands of men over the years, freely talk about their sex lives, it's obvious. Actually, it's comedic.

Once again, men are scum and proud of it. I include myself in the scum category, but strongly deny the kindergarten aspect.

There is perhaps, only one absolute truth in the universe.
And that is, whenever two or more men are together, there will be eventual, if not immediate "dirty talking."

The talk may involve a specific woman or just one walking by, on TV, an imaginary woman, or women in general. The talk ranges from suggestive to graphic and explicit to vulgar and ultimately refers to genitals.

Numerous male and female sources tell me that when women in some circles get together, the talk is even dirtier.

The tradition goes back to the 1300's, when code names were used to avoid impropriety. "Make a beast with two backs" was used in the 1300's. My best friend at the time asked me what she could do to make a guy fall in love with her. I advised her to talk dirty to him in bed during the act. .I recommended that she included fantasies he might like, as well as ones she liked. She was smart, creative, and daring. He married her.

The idea here and throughout this book is that the couple represents all men and all women everywhere.

Things no one ever wants to hear or say

It didn't mean anything

I'll never do it again

Please forgive me

It just happened

It wasn't my idea

I was drunk and didn't know what I was doing

I know you're seeing someone else

Are you in love with them?

I can't live with you anymore

How long has it been going on?

Where were you last night?

You don't love me anymore

You can just sleep on the couch

How could you betray me like this?

I want a divorce

Some Typical Man Stories

A man wakes up in the morning after a one-night stand. He finds the woman still asleep lying across his arm.

In order to leave silently without waking her.....he chews his arm off.

A guy said he always called his wife 20 minutes before he got home. He said it was a subtle warning to her, in case the mythical "Billy Bob" was there with her.

The guy reasoned if Billy Bob was there, the guy didn't want to know. And for sure didn't want his wife to know that he knew. And he was real sure that he didn't want to catch them in the act.

He was a smart guy that really loved his wife.

Another guy had been out all night screwing around. He came home early in the morning and his wife caught him coming in. She asked where he'd been.

He said it was such a warm night that he slept outside in the hammock. She said you know we got rid of that hammock last year.

He said, "Well, that's my story and I'm sticking to it.

A woman briefly noticed her husband on the phone in another room. Later she asked him who he was talking to.

He said it was some guy who had the wrong number and that they just got to talking.

Jealousy

Is flirting cheating? Is slow dancing with another cheating? What about smiling to a stranger; staring at a stranger; talking and laughing with a stranger; are any of these cheating?

They probably aren't cheating to the "letter" of the law. However, they may be strong indications of inner fantasies to have a sexual encounter with another.

Are they reasons for jealousy and resentment? Many people think so. Jealousy and negative reactions are ugly, but very preventable.

It has been said, "I like my mate being jealous." Really?
Do they enjoy yelling and screaming and arguing and hitting, possibly leading to violence, revenge, maybe even divorce?

Almost all people love to flirt and be flirted with. It's Nature's way and in the DNA. Jealousy is society's way. Jealousy is dangerous and unnecessary. If the soulmates simply accept each other's sexual nature and uninhibitedly enjoy it together, sexual peace of mind can easily be achieved.

"Monogamous promiscuity" Repeat that phrase over and over. Make it part of your vocabulary.

No Man Alive

No man alive or that ever has been alive, has not worried or at least, thought of or considered the possibility of another man screwing his wife. The same is true for a woman.

By accepting my proposal of "monogamous promiscuity," a wonderful "sexual peace of mind" will bless both partners.
They will never need to suffer from jealousy or mistrust again.

The concept of marriage, which is two people living as one, is now a sexual truism.

No Competition

After the couple has united in what I call monogamous promiscuity, there is no need to worry about their mate's emotional faithfulness. Consequently, the man does not have to compete with all other men in the world. Neither does the woman have to compete with all other women.

The threat of a harsh negative reaction or a break up for what used to be a sexual indiscretion has been removed. A mutual peace of mind has replaced it. Both know now, nothing can come between them.

What man in his right mind would ever leave a woman that loved him completely and also allowed him sexual freedom. What woman would ever leave a man that felt the same about her.

Very, very, very, seldom would either of them develop any kind of intimate feelings for someone else. They would have to be crazy.

RELAX; take it easy, you are both ONE with the other now!!!

Ménage a trois

I heard this story from a very reliable source and then verified it from another very reliable source. It is relevant to the discussion. It refers only to the physical act and not to the original French romantic arrangement.

A woman was curious and desired to be with two men sexually at the same time. She had asked her husband about it for a couple of years and he finally agreed to investigate the adventure for real.

The woman verbally communicated with several men on a dating service and eventually chose a man sight unseen. She didn't even ask for a picture, but she did speak with him on the phone two times.

She then arranged for her husband and the chosen man to have a phone conversation while she listened in. Her husband was obviously hesitant, not knowing how this might affect their future relationship.

Beginning the conversation was awkward. Then, her husband asked a dozen questions and then made a dozen rules. The man conformed to her husband's criteria, as she knew he would. The man conformed to her criteria also. She had vetted him beforehand.

The man agreed to her husband's requirements: there would be no kissing, no touching here, no touching there, no talking during the act, no eye contact, no Terms of Endearment afterward and no being in the same bed with her at the same time. Everyone agreed.

The three of them agreed to meet at a certain motel in a week. God only knows how much passion and lust they shared anticipating this forbidden new adventure. I am sure he was apprehensive and that she was confident it would create a brand new world for them.

Judgement day arrived. They rented a room with two beds. She was beautiful. The two men were good looking. Intense excitement and uncertainty abounded. It began.

She seductively initiated the encounter. She turned to her husband and sensually kissed him, then turned to the strange man and began the foreplay. Soon, she was having the multiple orgasms of "EVE."

She went from one bed to the other, then back and forth and back and forth, until she had satisfied her longed for lustful desires. When the Tempest had passed and they both realized there was no catastrophe, but rather a brand new beginning of future euphoria for man and wife, she turned to both men and said,

"Now that wasn't so bad and horrible for you two big strong scared boys, now was it???"

And that's what we're talking about. What man would ever leave a woman like that, knowing she would gladly reciprocate in his lustful desires? What woman would ever leave a man like that, willing to please her in every way?

Word has it that they are much more in love than ever. They are ecstatic.

And Finally

An 80 year old woman walks into an all-male rest home. There she encounters a group of men.

She exclaims, "if any one of you can tell me what I'm holding in my hand, he can make mad passionate love to me all night.

A man in the back responds, "an elephant."

The woman says..." that's close enough."

At last, what is the one conclusion that can be drawn from this book? Simply put, in order for both partners to achieve sexual peace of mind, they must first admit and accept the irrefutable universal law of sexual nature. Mother Nature did carve that law in stone thousands of years ago,

Once that has been accomplished, the concept of "cheating" no longer exists. More importantly, the "jealousy" that accompanies that concept is disarmed up front. Consequently, both partners realize that so called cheating is, has been, and ever will be going on, in both their minds. But now, it will go on together, but not labeled as cheating.

They can now enjoy each other's fantasies and or individual freedoms together. They can enjoy that bliss, whether they simply choose to enjoy it in their heads or actually decide to experience real sexual escapades.

Everything is out in the open now. Anything can be expressed without fear of reprisal. Both, can now reveal their innermost sexual desires. This private sacred conspiracy between the couple will bond them like no other.

This approach could easily lead both down the pathway to sweet sexual peace of mind. Good Luck!!!

POEMS BY THE AUTHOR RELEVANT TO THE THEME OF THE BOOK

One Foot Down and Dirty

One foot down and dirty
Yet that foot is free
To stand up strong and study
Find and fill a destiny

Now that I have over elaborated my enthusiasm to laugh and play with the decadent Goddess Queen in an experimental infinite game of pure freedom, daring adventure, and multi-leveled love, I turn my attention to your total amusement. Of course by now, you could realize why you deserve above all other women that I have ever met, to be worth of such esteem and privileged treatment. But in the event you do not yet recognize your special superiority and remain suspicious of my seemingly hasty conclusions, allow me to provide some poetic insights.

She said I was way ahead of her in feelings
She meant that I was impatient and naïve
She feared for the safety of her privacy or
That I was lying or had something up my sleeve

I understood her concerns, they were normal
Men have always injured women in their greed
And their lust and obsession for dominance
With selfish ego and insecurity, mind and deed

But her feelings did equal mine in intuition
We had both hoped and knew of what could be
An unconditional love between a man and a woman
Rich emotion, no negatives, both still free

To fully experience this earth dream
To learn from its pleasure and pain
Experiment with new and strange thinking
An inner glowing from individual gain

We both always thought it was possible
But at least I had never found a girl
Worthy or willing to risk the daring
Wise and smart enough to take the whirl

And I had looked in all kinds of places
Searching for this woman of great mind
Wishing to encounter just one equal
Knowing her rare treasure should I find

This female of like understanding
This woman of vision and sight
A Goddess to share illumination
A heroine of delicious delight

Sometimes I thought my idea quite evil
Other times, I laughed at its depravity
But always, it drove me with passion
Fill the void, cross the empty cavity

Span the cavern of unknown discovery
With a woman as wicked as me
A dark sided temptress, but loving
A female as pure as can be

To share perverted pleasure and daring
And to laugh at the mystery of life
Be unafraid to challenge blind ritual
Create joyful meaning from strife

Explore alternative explanations
Worship the dark as well as the light
Submit to the power of sensual urges
Feel the love of spiritual flight

Without guilt, without rationalization
Using only free will and mind
A bi-sexual oneness of spirit
Curious frolic for two of a kind

One of a kind with two bodies
One precious soul with two halves
Joining to form a completeness
One road that splits in two paths

The symbolic duality of yin/yang
Opposite in nature, but the same
Removing the illusion of difference
Resolving the harsh jealousy game

One wishing well for the other
No matter what lustful deed done
Understanding that freedom is beauty
That male/female conscious is one

Meant for an intimate sharing
Designed so when joined, they can see
A much greater human glory
A far more liberating ecstasy

Isn't this true love? I ask you
Every man and woman's possible bliss?
For transcending resentment of difference
For not fearing the abominable abyss

Of insecurity, pain, and rejection
Sensitivity of personal pride
The constraining chain of possession
A collar and leash to guide

I want to ask of you also
Do you not full concur with me?
Have I misjudged your wonder?
Aren't you exactly the way I see?

If so, you can see why I dearly love you
And now you know better what that phrase means
You know also how well we could taste life
Eat the sweet forbidden fruit of prurient dreams

But even if the fruit is forsaken
Not ripe from the heat of your sun
I still need the seeds of laughter
From the Goddess of decadent fun

Dream World

If there were a dream world,
Without a consequence.
A place of only present,
No past, no future to quench.

I'd insist we go there together,
For an hour or two or three,
To capture all your thrilling charms,
Sensual surrender's depravity.

Hot pleasure would I gift you,
The kind that is so rare.
The quiver of the kinky,
Would grace your skin so fair.

The scream of primal urges,
Would issue from your soul.
Seduction of a Goddess,
Male and female; whole.

The nakedness of beauty.
The mystery revealed.
The joys of the body,
Nothing left concealed.

The chains of social custom,
Would lack their prison force.
The cuffs of inhibition,
Void of mental source.

Only desire of men and women.
We would represent them all;
The passion of the difference,
Their union before the Fall.

The sacred Eve of Adam.
The truth of He and She.
The risk of total pleasure,
Our wickedness to free.

To fill the wanton abyss.
To cross to the other side.
To worship in the Oneness,
To force the hesitant bride.

Free her from her devil,
Alleviate her guilt.
Allow her to be equal.
Love her to the hilt.

Be it touch or taste or vision,
Sound or perfumed smell.
Glorify her being,
Eliminate her hell.

Conjugate sex power,
Feel it deep inside.
Helpless in the miracle,
Nothing left to hide.

If there were a dream world, without a conscious cost,
I'd force you to go with me, regain sweet paradise lost.

GODDESS

Never met a girl names Goddess before.
Looked at her face then stared at her more.
In her voice, the joy of feminine laughter,
Sharing dark ironic humor, her as my master.

The cosmic joke of life to tell,
Our different version of heaven and hell.
Heaven and hell and which is which?
Mystery of mind, so strange so rich.

Body and soul the same to see.
One is dying, the other free.
What's their connection upon this earth,
A mystical illusion of ironic mirth?

Psychological punishment, tragedy,
The result of socialized tyranny?
Or does it go beyond the state,
To inner self and human fate?

Does destiny play the major part?
Or is freewill left to guide the heart?
If I can choose freewill to please,
The love of self, I'll gladly seize.

And when myself is understood,
I'll move my quest to womanhood.
Great magic can thrive between the sexes,
But no other inhibition, so severely vexes.

Man and woman, the mysterious jolt.
Joy to them, it's natures bolt.

And when their shame's at last removed,
Then sacred meaning can be resumed.

As it was with Eve in that playful place,
Without guilt and fear and social race.
Eve's deception was a broad face lie.
It needs correction, it needs to die.

A world without a Goddess is a desolate sphere,
Full of hatred and violence, torment and tear.
Where has gone wisdom? Where has gone love?
Looked for in maleness, looked for above.

Never looked inward, never chose Her as One.
Took it all too serious, overlooked the fun.
Female Deity close inside the self,
Miracle and magic, abundant mental wealth.

Repression, suppression, a myth for fools.
With power and truth, the Goddess rules.
She rules the night. She rules the day.
In beauty and love, she lights the way.

Her fire of justice, equal and fair.
Burns hot to touch and begs to share,
The gift of oneness, the union of twins,
The error of separation, the lie of sins.

The male and female are opposite halves,
Of a splendid glory, not separate paths.
One to worship, the other to shun?
One to dominate and the world to run?

One subservient to a Maker's touch?
How stupid and cruel and evil as such.
Were I to choose which superior to be.
The giver of breath, it appears to me.

The Goddess rules the throne of life.
Without Her presence, an awful strife.
Which's what the Earth has come to be,
An insane and ruthless conspiracy.

Never met a Goddess named Woman before.
Looked at her face, then stared at her more.
Her beauty is exquisite, her presence just right.
Her body and being, the most wonderful sight.

Worship and praise, the altar of high.
Consciousness raise and ignorance die.

A pleasant surprise of laughter and mirth,
A philosophical view of refreshing rebirth.
An alluring creature with positive mind.
A beautiful woman I am encouraged to find.

Not afraid of questions with a devious wit,
Full of challenge and energy of perfect fit.
Confident, competent, sure of her queendom.
A feminine woman, not cumbered by king dumb.

Moonlight

The forces of the moon, waxing waning.
The forces of nature changing straining.
The nature of Man, blaming, blaming.
The predicament of His plight.

You and I yearning burning,
To express our being, love and learning.
Who will listen now?

Caste of doubt and guilt and anguish,
Who and what will fears extinguish?
Who and what and where and how?

Driven inward, driven outward.
Question North and question southward,
Any and everywhere the answers lie.

And lie they do in every action,
Every thought of every faction,
The true and false of meaning vie.

What is true and good and sacred,
What is false and filled with hatred,
Lie within us all.

Can we grasp the truth and recover?
Open to the mystery and pleasure of a lover?
Or was that all lost in the original Fall?

Is Eden's bliss of innocence ended?
Its pain of rejection forever extended,
To an eternity of pain and guilt?

Or are we will within its borders,
Safe from harm, awaiting orders,
To have fun, a free and happy tilt?

No one knows, it is not certain.
We cannot see beyond the curtain,
Behind which our beauty lies.

Wisdom of the "PRESENT"

The joy of "to be" is the present.
The thrill of alive is the right now.
The thought of "you" is quite pleasant.
No need to derive "why and how."

I'm drinking of the Cup of pure pleasure.
I'm drunk from the touch of your wine.
The mystery of your sweet female treasure,
Clings softly on me, wrapping vine.

Why mention the question of love/lust?
The soul or the body to shun.
The two share a definition of same trust.
Which one the light, which the sun?

Which the before, which the after?
Eventually both will have been one.
Why worry or fret future disaster?
Live now. Too soon, life is done.

I'm thinking of your sweet female sweetness.
The sweetest taste drips from my lips.
Today, tomorrow, thereafter,
From the Cup may we both choose our sips.

The Dilemma

The French in all their glory
Of cabaret lure, and mirth
Cannot match the splendor
Of innocent love's rebirth

Kissing, touching carefully
Afraid of sensual flame
Knowing of its grandeur
But fearful of its shame

Protecting hidden secrets
From sight and mind and taste
Forbidding their exposure
And submission gained thru haste

Both know of the pleasure
They too have felt the pain
A heaven and hell sensation
Of the lust and lost refrain

Of a never ending process
The song of new sexual joy
Discover of virgin emotion
Twin magic of a girl and boy

Attraction burns so brightly
Cannot resist its heat
A natural glowing of oneness
Male/female body to meet

Both quake from the danger
Thrill of the taboo ground
Quiver with risky excitement
And the lover they have found

But never forgetting the downside
Knowing what is over that crest
Remembering the past exploitation
Rejection, the suffering, the rest.

But still the urge to go forward
The suicidal instinct to join
A pact for sharing pain/pleasure
To pocket the two sided coin.

A dare to merge with their difference
A hope to understand what's desired
The hopeless pursuit of completeness
Regardless what the past has transpired

A need to share definition of meaning
To bare the soul, the body, the mind
No matter the cost or what the jeopardy
For passion of the sexes entwined

And the force that drives them crazy
Is planted deep inside
And it yearns to express its secrets
Does not desire to hide

Longs to be accepted
Begs to be set free
Beckons to be honored
Acknowledged as deity

Master of this earth plane
Ruler of sacred and good
Holy inner burning fire
Suppressed, misunderstood

The two can see that vision
If only for awhile
The rapture of sweet reunion
Then back into exile

Their bodies growing nearer
To touch and blend what's right
To resurrect the spirit
And reconjure creation's might

The innocence of new lovers
Yielding to temptation's power
Wishing giving only pleasure
As the scented sight of flower

Lips on lips and naked
Ecstasy's perfect fit
Union of knowing oneness
Love in the fiery pit

A Wish

Voice of Venus rising
Music in my ears
Melody so surprising
Eases sexual fears

A goddess of redemption
The queen of feminine bliss
Beauty without exemption
Power of innocent kiss

Woman beyond just body
Female of purest soul
Let me view the grandeur
Show me spirit's whole

Show me platonic friendship
With a hint of sweet prurient delight
Tease me with your visual wonder
Allow me to imagine its glorious sight

Laugh and play with me in the garden
Instruct me in natural fun
Remove the conditioned barriers
Communicate with me as one

Being not afraid of our difference
Still enjoying the spark of its flare
But retaining the privilege of freedom
And the unconventional wisdom of "to dare"

Reveal the truth of what's hidden
The glow of your inner mind's self
Risk for the rapture of sharing
The goodness of our spiritual wealth

For the soul of the goddess is in you
You burn bright from her presence of light
You are blessed with the "mystery of woman"
Worth of worship, the phoenix in flight

Blazing from love's true essence
On fire with future dream
Knowing of self fulfilment
Feeling your consciousness stream

Permit me be your mirror
Reflect your truth, your joy
A simple natural friendship
of a curious girl and boy

The Truth Of It

You truly are... unlike any other
And you brave an association with me
My attempt is to discretely discover
The what and illusive why of the we

The edge and the dare of the dark side
The joy and the laughter of the light
The trust and the courage to confide
The excitement and adventure of the night

Two opposites of gender and body
Yet the same soul of spirit and mind
The combination of innocence and naughty
But the recognition of playful like kind

The yin/yang of youth and of aging
The breathtaking thrill of taboo
A sweet union of sorts, so engaging
Both our sensual energies to renew

Perhaps not in a conventional lifestyle
Nor on a stage of fireworks and flame
But a secret lust of mutual worthwhile
Maybe an imaginary fantasy to reclaim

Of course, that is the juice of male/female
That is their fruit and their pain
Forever separate "twins" destined to fail, re-fail
Pleasure/passion but no further gain

But as unlikely and unlike as you are
And as uniquely unorthodox as I
A hope that we might together go far
In establishing the truth of the why

The Self and the Mated Self

To breathe and live,
Is question and wonder?
At beauty beheld,
Storm and thunder.

Life's answers lie,
In the deep blue sea,
The painted sky,
A wish to be free

Freedom is sacred.
Freedom is rare.
Freedom of thought,
With courage to dare.

The karma of the process,
The inner growing pain.
Knowledge of the Giver,
The fruit of human gain.

Our purpose was from the beginning,
To bear the Spirit's blood,
To create order from chaotic spinning,
To build on Foundation's stud.

According to each one's talent,
Is the individual's rule.
To work and learn and love Earth,
To seek the personal jewel.

Do what thou will and be happy.
Seek your bliss, you'll be fine.
Contribute to the Great Work in your way,
Cut your own path, I'll cut mine.

The tale of punishment stories,
To frighten us to join the herd,
And sacrifice heaven's glories,
Is superstition, in place of the Word.

Now, the Word is quite a concept.
The gift of knowledge, a greater high.
We're still standing in the Garden.
Look around, breathe a welcome sigh.

The gospel is a postlude.
To the more brutal original script.
The good news is our Oneness,
Of that, we can't be stripped.

But it is up to each to enjoy It,
To find their own special way,
To serve a part in love and freedom,
Be alive, fear not what they say.

"For they know not what they do."

Just South of Heaven

Just beyond the boundary where reality breeds illusion.
Just south of heaven I live in a blissful exclusion.

Just beyond the limit, not far outside the gate,
I walk in personal freedom, a lovely chosen state.

I lived inside the border in the younger years.
And shared insane beliefs of many anguished peers.

But I escaped the cloning threat,
Fought my fear, made my bet.

That every social ritual was in itself a lie.
Happiness, peace, and meaning, I knew I could not buy.

Realizing this futility of continued false purpose,
I ponder my options to break free of this surface.

Neither commune, hermit, nor death did I want.
I was finally resigned to take a scary daring jaunt!

I walked to the edge, then took a big leap,
Into a vast unknown both strange and deep.

I landed just south of heaven in a place called Mind,
A place with no guild or worry, but rather difficult to find.

It does not exist on a conventional map.
I let go of direction and fell in its lap.

A lap of pure plenty and a lap of pure glee,
Everything there's just to satisfy me.

Being truly amazed at the extent of its wonder;
Of beauty and love and creative thunder,

I share it with One. Would share it with All.
Haven of The Source, I revere it with awe.

Land of sweet infinite, home of all time.
Everything improving within perfect rhyme.

Better and better, this shelter evolves,
Questions and problems, dilemmas resolves.

Discovery and learning in this timeless place.
Synchronicity churning, self-truth to be faced.

I am living just south of heaven in a place called Mind,
Offering bliss and contentment, but it's not easy to find.

A blind jump is needed to find its location;
To explore hidden paths; to find inspiration.

It takes courage to jump, not how far or wide,
Takes the wisdom to trust and faith to let guide.

Life's Questions

What is there to learn and why?
Who will teach me what?
When will I know, "Who am I?"
How will I be taught?

How easy are life's lessons?
Where am I to look?
Are they simply classroom sessions?
Is wisdom found in books?

What is my reflection?
How do I relate?
Linked to Introspection?
Or chained to social state?

Is learning really knowing?
Is knowledge all that great?
What's my character showing?
What will be my fate?

Who will be my partners?
What will we achieve?
Must we be mass martyrs?
What will we believe?

Why will we believe it?
Who will force us then?
Can we choose our own wit?
Will the still be sin?

Can I rise above me?
Will I know what's good?
Will people always love me?
Can I imagine "could?"

When will I feel confidence?
When will I love "me?"
Am I doomed to reticence?
When will I be free?

Who will give me freedom?
What unlocks that door?
Knowledge the sweet medium?
If so, can I seek more?

Where can I find honor?
Where does truth's worth lie?
Will I be a "conner?"
Or set my standards high?

Answers lie in questions.
Answers always have.
Inner query destines.
The individual path.

It's always my decision.
To choose which road and why.
I'm free to make revision.
I'm free to touch the sky.

Time—Better Enjoy It

Time is a killer concept,
But it's really all we have.
It's what we sell and bargain for,
And serves as healing salve.

To ease the pain of memory,
To nullify the past.
A hope for in the future.
A gauge of first to last.

And when that last is present,
No hope for any more,
No span of life immortal,
Only wish eternity's shore.

It's up to us to use it.
To use it the best we can.
There's just a fleeting second,
Before that permanent ban.

Time is growing nearer,
Shorter toward the end.
Cannot save its going,
Save its power to mend.

Cannot keep its wonder,
A treasure to be stored.
Precious seconds wasting,
No time to be bored.

Live its worth completely
All one has is now.
Savor every moment.
Never question how.

Joyously spend the present.
Purchase freely, as you go.
Worship in its lasting.
Time's your friend and of course your foe.

About the Author

The author is well educated, well-traveled, and well experienced. He is a graduate Marshall University with a minor in philosophy. Since then, he has studied and researched many different philosophies, cultures, and religions. He was a teenager in the 60's, the era of "sex, drugs, and rock n roll." The sexual revolution was dramatic and explosive in those times and has progressed to the present.

From a lifelong career in sales, including computers and real estate, as well as other products and services, he has met and communicated with thousands of people. He has socialized with the very rich and the very poor. He has served as a speaker and a writer, self-circulating his observations of life in his compositions of "Vic's Friend," in the 70's and 80's.

In addition, his experience with other people he has met in the course of casual socialization has added many insights and perspectives. His associations with random other people include sports, poker, golf, classes, bar hopping, cocktail parties, even church. All of these activities and more allowed him to be privy to secret confessions, off hand remarks, candid viewpoints, and constant over and over references to sex.

Through quite a few various dating services, he has had phone conversations and dialogue with five to six hundred different women across the USA. Those conversations provided more personal insights and perspectives. Some of those were explicit. Some were graphic. All were sexually enlightening.

He is convinced, perhaps along with Sigmund Freud, that sex is the overwhelming driving force of the human mind. It is the major preoccupation of the vast majority of people, along with money. He is convinced that sex and money are the great motivators of civilization itself.

Obviously, the author acknowledges his preoccupation and believes the same instincts reside in the minds all adult humans, whether they will admit it or not.

As a graduate of Silva Mind Control, the author is a strong proponent of alpha thinking, imagination, and freedom of thought, action, and behavior. Through the years, he has attempted to encourage all people to use the awesome untapped powers of the individual human mind to create new realities for themselves. The author believes the possibilities for the individual are boundless and for a completely unified couple, even more boundless, possibly infinite.

Printed in the United States
By Bookmasters